Mindful Living: Cultivating Inner Peace in a Busy World

1. --
2. Summary
3. Chapter 2
4. Chapter 1: Introduction to Mindfulness
5. Chapter 2: Historical Journey of Mindfulness
6. Chapter 3: The Art of Starting: Basics of Mindful Living
7. Chapter 4: Mindful Eating and Movement
8. Chapter 5: Enhancing Communication through Mindfulness
9. Chapter 6: Transforming Work Habits with Mindfulness
10. Chapter 7: Nurturing Relationships through Mindful Practices
11. Chapter 8: Advanced Practices in Mindfulness
12. Chapter 9: Extending the Practice Beyond the Self
13. Chapter 10: Special Techniques and Approaches in Mindful Living
14. Chapter 11: Overcoming Obstacles in Advanced Practice
15. Chapter 12: Continuing the Journey – Lifelong Practice
16. Synopsis

Summary

Chapter 1: Introduction to Mindfulness   3
1.1 The Modern Need for Mindfulness   3
1.2 Understanding Mindfulness: Definitions and Benefits   5
1.3 The Science Behind Mindfulness: Mental Health and Productivity   7
Chapter 2: Historical Journey of Mindfulness   9
2.1 From Eastern Origins to Western Integration   9
2.2 Philosophical Foundations of Mindfulness Practices   1:
2.3 The Role of Meditation in Mindfulness   1:
Chapter 3: The Art of Starting: Basics of Mindful Living   1:
3.1 Establishing a Personal Practice   1:
3.2 Overcoming Common Challenges and Misconceptions   1'
3.3 Creating a Mindful Environment   1!
Chapter 4: Mindful Eating and Movement   2
4.1 Cultivating Awareness in Eating Habits   2
4.2 Integrating Mindfulness into Physical Activity   2:
4.3 Mindful Eating for Better Health   2:
Chapter 5: Enhancing Communication through Mindfulness   2'
5.1 Listening with Full Attention   2'
5.2 Speaking with Purpose and Kindness   2!
5.3 Mindful Communication in Relationships   3
Chapter 6: Transforming Work Habits with Mindfulness   3:
6.1 Creating a Balanced Work-Life through Presence   3:
6.2 Managing Stress and Enhancing Productivity   3:
6.3 Mindful Leadership and Teamwork   3'

Chapter 7: Nurturing Relationships through Mindful Practices
7.1 Deepening Connections with Others
7.2 Handling Conflicts with Compassion
7.3 Building Empathy and Understanding
Chapter 8: Advanced Practices in Mindfulness
8.1 Developing Compassion and Empathy
8.2 Using Mindfulness to Navigate Difficult Emotions
8.3 Cultivating Gratitude and Forgiveness
Chapter 9: Extending the Practice Beyond the Self
9.1 Impacting the Community Positively
9.2 Environmental Consciousness through Mindful Living
9.3 Mindfulness in Education and Social Change
Chapter 10: Special Techniques and Approaches in Mindful Living
10.1 Exploring Various Meditation Techniques
10.2 Tailoring Practices to Individual Needs
10.3 Mindfulness in Daily Activities
Chapter 11: Overcoming Obstacles in Advanced Practice
11.1 Dealing with Plateaus in Practice
11.2 Addressing Advanced Challenges
11.3 Maintaining Motivation and Consistency
Chapter 12: Continuing the Journey – Lifelong Practice
12.1 Incorporating Lessons into Daily Life
12.2 Resources for Further Exploration
12.3 Sustaining a Mindful Lifestyle

1 Introduction to Mindfulness

1.1 The Modern Need for Mindfulness

In today's fast-paced world, the concept of mindfulness has transitioned from a traditional practice to a necessary tool for navigating the complexities of modern life. The escalating pace at which we live, work, and interact with technology has led to an increase in stress and anxiety levels, making mindfulness more relevant than ever. This section delves into why mindfulness is not just beneficial but essential in our current era.

The constant connectivity enabled by smartphones and the internet means that we are rarely disconnected from our work or social networks. This perpetual state of alertness can lead to digital fatigue, a phenomenon where individuals feel overwhelmed by the amount of digital communication they are exposed to. Mindfulness offers a way to counteract this overload by encouraging moments of pause, reflection, and connection with the present moment.

Moreover, the modern workplace often demands multitasking and high productivity levels, contributing to increased stress and burnout rates among professionals. Mindfulness practices can enhance focus and productivity while reducing stress by teaching individuals how to manage their attention more effectively. By cultivating a mindful approach to work and life, people can improve their mental health and overall well-being.

The rise in mental health awareness has also highlighted the need for accessible tools that support emotional well-being. Mindfulness has been scientifically proven to reduce symptoms of anxiety and depression, making it a valuable resource for those seeking non-pharmacological interventions.

Its adaptability across different cultures and demographics further underscores its significance in addressing global mental health challenges.

Mindfulness as a response to digital overload

Enhancing focus in multitasking environments

Supporting mental health in an age of increasing awareness

In conclusion, the modern need for mindfulness is driven by our rapidly changing world, characterized by technological advancements and evolving workplace dynamics. By integrating mindfulness into daily routines, individuals can navigate these challenges with greater resilience, clarity, and peace. As we continue to face new stresses and distractions, mindfulness stands out as a timeless practice that offers profound benefits for contemporary society.

1.2 Understanding Mindfulness: Definitions and Benefits

Mindfulness, a term that has seen its popularity soar in contemporary discourse, is often associated with mental well-being, stress reduction, and enhanced focus. At its core, mindfulness is the practice of being fully present and engaged in the moment, aware of our thoughts and feelings without distraction or judgment. This section explores the multifaceted definitions of mindfulness and delves into its numerous benefits for individuals navigating the complexities of modern life.

The roots of mindfulness can be traced back to ancient practices, particularly within Buddhist traditions where it is considered a key step towards enlightenment. However, in the Western context, mindfulness has been secularized and adapted for therapeutic purposes. Jon Kabat-Zinn, a pioneer in this field, defines mindfulness as "the awareness that arises from paying attention, on purpose, in the present moment and non-judgmentally."

This definition underscores the importance of intentionality and acceptance in the practice of mindfulness.

Engaging in mindfulness practices offers a plethora of benefits that address both mental and physical health concerns. Psychologically, it has been shown to reduce symptoms of anxiety and depression by breaking down patterns of negative thinking and rumination. Mindfulness encourages an attitude of openness and curiosity about one's experiences, which can lead to greater emotional resilience.

From a physiological perspective, regular mindfulness practice has been linked to lower blood pressure, improved sleep quality, and enhanced immune function. These benefits are thought to arise from mindfulness' ability to reduce stress-related responses in the body which are often at the root of various health issues.

In addition to health benefits, mindfulness also enhances cognitive functions such as attention span, memory retention, and decision-making skills. By training the mind to focus on the present moment without distraction, individuals can improve their performance in both personal and professional spheres.

The adaptability of mindfulness across different cultures and demographics further amplifies its appeal as a universal tool for enhancing well-being. Whether practiced through formal meditation or integrated into daily activities like eating or walking, mindfulness offers a pathway towards living more consciously and fully engaged with life's experiences.

In conclusion, understanding mindfulness involves recognizing its rich historical origins as well as appreciating its broad application today. The benefits of adopting a mindful approach to life are extensive—ranging from improved mental health to better physical well-being—and underscore why this ancient practice remains profoundly relevant in our modern world.

1.3 The Science Behind Mindfulness: Mental Health and Productivity

The burgeoning interest in mindfulness within the scientific community has led to a significant body of research exploring its effects on mental health and productivity. This surge in empirical evidence provides a robust framework for understanding how mindfulness practices can lead to tangible benefits in these areas. By delving into the mechanisms through which mindfulness operates, we can appreciate its potential as a powerful tool for enhancing well-being and efficiency in our daily lives.

Mindfulness meditation, characterized by its emphasis on present-moment awareness and non-judgmental observation, has been shown to effect changes in various areas of the brain associated with attention, emotion regulation, and self-awareness. Studies utilizing functional magnetic resonance imaging (fMRI) have observed increased activity in the prefrontal cortex, an area linked to higher-order brain functions such as decision-making and concentration. Concurrently, there is a decrease in activity within the amygdala, known for its role in stress responses. These neural changes not only contribute to reduced symptoms of anxiety and depression but also enhance cognitive capabilities that are crucial for productivity.

From a mental health perspective, mindfulness-based interventions (MBIs) like Mindfulness-Based Stress Reduction (MBSR) have demonstrated efficacy in reducing symptoms of various psychological disorders including anxiety, depression, and post-traumatic stress disorder (PTSD). By fostering an attitude of acceptance towards one's thoughts and feelings rather than avoidance or over-engagement, individuals learn to disengage from maladaptive patterns of rumination and worry that often underlie these conditions.

In terms of productivity, the practice of mindfulness has been linked with improved attention span and memory retention. The ability to maintain focus on the task at hand without succumbing to distractions is essential in today's fast-paced world where multitasking is common yet counterproductive. Furthermore, mindfulness encourages a state of flow—a highly focused mental state conducive to creativity and efficiency—thereby enhancing performance across various domains.

Moreover, mindfulness practices have been associated with better decision-making skills. By cultivating a heightened awareness of one's thought processes and emotional states, individuals are better equipped to make reasoned choices rather than impulsive decisions based on transient emotions or external pressures.

In conclusion, the science behind mindfulness offers compelling evidence for its benefits regarding mental health and productivity. Through regular practice, individuals can foster greater emotional resilience and unlock their full potential for focus and efficiency. As research continues to unravel the complexities of how mindfulness affects the brain and behavior, it becomes increasingly clear why this ancient practice holds significant relevance for our contemporary lives.

2 Historical Journey of Mindfulness

2.1 From Eastern Origins to Western Integration

The journey of mindfulness from its Eastern origins to Western integration is a fascinating tale of cultural exchange, scientific curiosity, and the universal quest for inner peace. This narrative not only highlights the adaptability and resilience of mindfulness as a practice but also underscores the interconnectedness of human experiences across different cultures and epochs.

Mindfulness, with its roots deeply embedded in ancient Buddhist, Hindu, and Taoist traditions, was primarily concerned with spiritual awakening and enlightenment. It was an integral part of meditative practices designed to cultivate awareness, compassion, and insight into the nature of existence. The philosophical foundations laid by these traditions provided a rich tapestry of techniques and insights that have been refined over millennia.

The transition of mindfulness into Western consciousness began with explorers, missionaries, and scholars who encountered these Eastern practices during their travels. However, it wasn't until the late 20th century that mindfulness morphed from a niche interest into a mainstream phenomenon in Western societies. This shift can largely be attributed to pioneering individuals like Jon Kabat-Zinn, whose work at the University of Massachusetts Medical School introduced mindfulness as a secular form of stress reduction—Mindfulness-Based Stress Reduction (MBSR). Kabat-Zinn's efforts to strip mindfulness of its religious connotations without diluting its essence made it accessible to a broader audience.

In conclusion, the journey from Eastern origins to Western integration illustrates how mindfulness has transcended cultural boundaries to become a global phenomenon. By adapting traditional wisdom for contemporary needs while maintaining its core principles, mindfulness continues to offer sanctuary for those seeking solace in today's tumultuous times.

Scientific research played a crucial role in this cultural assimilation process. As studies began to empirically demonstrate the benefits of mindfulness on mental health, cognitive function, and overall well-being, skepticism turned into curiosity among medical professionals and the general public alike. This growing body of evidence has been instrumental in integrating mindfulness into various aspects of Western life—from healthcare systems and educational institutions to corporate wellness programs.

Today's digital age has further democratized access to mindfulness through apps, online courses, and virtual retreats. These platforms offer guidance from seasoned practitioners across the globe, enabling anyone with internet access to explore this ancient practice. Despite its commercialization concerns, this digital proliferation underscores mindfulness's universal appeal—a testament to its potential for fostering greater empathy, resilience, and well-being in our fast-paced world.

2.2 Philosophical Foundations of Mindfulness Practices

The philosophical underpinnings of mindfulness practices are as diverse as they are profound, stretching across various Eastern traditions that have, over centuries, offered insights into the nature of mind and reality. At the heart of these philosophies is a shared emphasis on awareness, compassion, and the interconnectedness of all beings—a foundation that has allowed mindfulness to transcend cultural and temporal boundaries.

Buddhism, perhaps most famously associated with mindfulness, introduces it as part of the Eightfold Path to enlightenment. Here, mindfulness (Sati in Pali) is not merely a practice but a way of being that involves constant awareness of one's thoughts, feelings, and sensations without attachment or judgment. This tradition emphasizes the impermanence of all things (anicca), suffering (dukkha), and non-self (anatta) as core insights to be realized through mindful living.

Hinduism contributes to the tapestry of mindfulness through practices like yoga and meditation aimed at achieving moksha—liberation from the cycle of birth and death. The Bhagavad Gita elaborates on mindfulness by advocating for detached action (karma yoga) and meditation on the divine (bhakti yoga), highlighting self-awareness and devotion as paths toward spiritual awakening.

Taoism offers another perspective with its principle of Wu Wei—effortless action or action through non-action. This philosophy encourages flowing with life's natural rhythms in a state of deep awareness and harmony with the Tao (the Way). Mindfulness in this context is about aligning oneself with the spontaneity and simplicity of nature, embodying peace and flexibility in response to life's changes.

The integration of these philosophical foundations into Western thought has been facilitated by figures like Jon Kabat-Zinn, who distilled mindfulness into a secular practice accessible to people regardless of their religious or cultural background. By emphasizing mindfulness's universal applicability for reducing stress and enhancing well-being, its essence has been preserved while adapting to contemporary needs.

Scientific research further bridges East and West by validating ancient wisdom through empirical evidence. Studies on Mindfulness-Based Stress Reduction (MBSR) and other similar programs demonstrate significant benefits for mental health, cognitive function, and physical well-being. This convergence of philosophy, science, and practical application illustrates how deeply interconnected our quest for understanding the mind truly is across different cultures.

In conclusion, the philosophical foundations of mindfulness practices offer rich insights into human consciousness that are both timeless and universally relevant. By exploring these roots, we can appreciate mindfulness not just as a technique for personal development but as a profound expression of humanity's collective search for meaning and connection.

2.3 The Role of Meditation in Mindfulness

The practice of meditation is central to the cultivation and understanding of mindfulness, serving as both a foundational tool and an ongoing method for deepening awareness. While mindfulness encompasses a broader spectrum of awareness and presence in every moment of life, meditation offers a structured pathway to develop these qualities. Through meditation, individuals learn to observe their thoughts, feelings, and bodily sensations without judgment, fostering a state of open attentiveness that is the hallmark of mindfulness.

Meditation practices vary widely across different traditions but share common objectives: to quiet the mind, enhance concentration, and promote emotional equilibrium. In the context of mindfulness, meditation is not merely about achieving temporary states of calm or relaxation but about transforming how we relate to our experiences. It encourages an intimate exploration of our mental processes, helping us recognize patterns that may contribute to stress and suffering.

Historically rooted in ancient spiritual traditions such as Buddhism, Hinduism, and Taoism—each offering its unique meditative techniques—

meditation has been integral to mindfulness from its inception. Buddhist Vipassana (insight) meditation, for example, emphasizes direct observation of one's moment-to-moment experience with a gentle acceptance. This practice aligns closely with the contemporary understanding of mindfulness as maintaining a moment-by-moment awareness.

In modern applications, secular forms of meditation such as Mindfulness-Based Stress Reduction (MBSR) have distilled these ancient practices into non-religious exercises aimed at reducing stress and improving well-being. These programs often begin with focused attention on the breath—a simple yet profound practice that anchors awareness in the present moment—and gradually expand into other areas such as mindful walking or eating.

The scientific community has shown increasing interest in meditation's role within mindfulness practices. Research demonstrates that regular meditation can lead to structural changes in the brain associated with enhanced attention, emotional regulation, and reduced reactivity to stressors. These findings underscore meditation's transformative potential not only as a practice for personal development but also as a therapeutic intervention for mental health.

In conclusion, meditation serves as both the foundation and the continuous thread woven through the fabric of mindfulness practices. By cultivating a disciplined yet gentle focus on our inner experiences, it teaches us to approach life with greater clarity, compassion, and equanimity. As we deepen our meditative practice, we unlock new dimensions of mindfulness that enrich our engagement with ourselves and the world around us.

The Art of Starting: Basics of Mindful Living

3.1 Establishing a Personal Practice

The journey towards mindful living begins with the establishment of a personal practice, a cornerstone for cultivating inner peace and resilience in today's fast-paced world. This foundational step is crucial for anyone seeking to integrate mindfulness into their daily life, offering a structured approach to developing self-awareness and emotional regulation. By dedicating time and effort to this practice, individuals can embark on a transformative path that enhances their mental health and overall well-being.

Creating a personal mindfulness practice involves more than just occasional meditation; it requires commitment, consistency, and an openness to explore various techniques that resonate with one's lifestyle and preferences. The beauty of mindfulness lies in its flexibility—there is no one-size-fits-all approach. Whether it's through guided meditations, mindful walking, or simply incorporating mindful moments throughout the day, each person can discover what best suits their needs.

To begin establishing a personal practice, setting realistic goals is essential. Starting with just a few minutes each day can lead to significant benefits over time. It's also helpful to create a dedicated space for practice—a quiet corner in your home where you can sit undisturbed. This physical space can serve as a reminder and motivator for daily practice.

Identify specific times of the day when you are most likely to be consistent with your practice.

Experiment with different mindfulness exercises to find what truly helps you connect with the present moment.

Keep track of your progress and feelings in a journal to reflect on your journey and adjust your practices as needed.

Overcoming challenges such as time constraints or skepticism requires patience and perseverance. Remember that mindfulness is not about achieving perfection but about embracing each moment with awareness and compassion. As you continue on this path, you'll likely notice subtle shifts in your reactions to stressors, an increased sense of calm in everyday situations, and an enhanced connection with yourself and others.

In conclusion, establishing a personal mindfulness practice is an empowering step towards leading a more conscious and fulfilling life. By integrating mindful habits into our daily routines, we open ourselves up to the profound benefits of increased clarity, emotional balance, and inner peace.

3.2 Overcoming Common Challenges and Misconceptions

The journey towards mindful living, while rewarding, is often fraught with challenges and misconceptions that can deter or derail individuals from establishing a consistent practice. Understanding and addressing these hurdles is crucial for anyone looking to deepen their mindfulness journey.

One of the most significant challenges faced by beginners is the misconception that mindfulness requires emptying the mind of thoughts. This misunderstanding can lead to frustration when individuals find themselves unable to achieve this impossible standard. In reality, mindfulness is about becoming an observer of one's thoughts without judgment, not eliminating them entirely. Emphasizing this distinction can help practitioners approach their practice with more compassion and patience.

Another common hurdle is the struggle to find time in one's daily schedule for mindfulness practices. The fast-paced nature of modern life means that carving out moments for stillness and reflection can seem like a daunting task. However, integrating mindfulness does not necessarily require long periods of meditation; it can be as simple as paying full attention to the sensations of breathing for a few minutes or being fully present during routine activities such as eating or walking. Highlighting the flexibility of mindfulness practices in fitting into various lifestyles can encourage more consistent engagement.

Misconceptions about the immediate effects of mindfulness also pose a challenge. Some individuals may expect quick fixes to deep-seated issues or significant life improvements in a short period. This expectation can lead to disappointment and disillusionment when results are not instantly noticeable. It's important to communicate that benefits from mindfulness accumulate over time through regular practice, offering gradual enhancements in well-being rather than instant solutions.

Lastly, skepticism towards mindfulness as a legitimate tool for mental health and well-being can deter some from even beginning their practice. This skepticism often stems from a lack of understanding or exposure to misrepresented information about what mindfulness entails and its scientifically backed benefits. Providing clear, evidence-based information on how mindfulness impacts the brain and improves various aspects of life can help overcome this barrier.

In conclusion, overcoming these common challenges and misconceptions requires patience, education, and persistence. By setting realistic expectations, integrating small mindful moments throughout the day, and emphasizing the science-backed benefits of practice, individuals can navigate these hurdles more effectively. Ultimately, this will enable them to establish a more fulfilling and sustainable personal mindfulness practice.

3.3 Creating a Mindful Environment

Creating a mindful environment is an essential step in fostering a sustainable mindfulness practice. This process involves curating your physical and mental spaces to support awareness, presence, and peace. By intentionally designing our surroundings, we can significantly enhance our ability to engage with the present moment, making mindfulness more accessible in our daily lives.

The foundation of creating a mindful environment lies in simplicity and intentionality. Clutter, whether physical or digital, can be a significant barrier to mindfulness, as it often leads to distraction and stress. Simplifying your space by decluttering and organizing can create a serene atmosphere that encourages focus and calmness. This doesn't mean living minimally but rather choosing to surround yourself with items that serve a purpose or bring joy, thereby reducing unnecessary distractions.

Nature plays a pivotal role in enhancing mindfulness. Incorporating elements of nature into your environment, such as plants, natural light, or even nature sounds can help ground you in the present moment. Studies have shown that exposure to natural environments significantly reduces stress and increases feelings of well-being. Even if access to outdoor spaces is limited, small changes like keeping a plant on your desk or using natural materials in decor can make a difference.

The use of color is another powerful tool in creating a mindful environment. Colors have the ability to influence our mood and cognitive function. For instance, blues and greens are often associated with calmness and concentration, making them excellent choices for spaces dedicated to meditation or reflection. On the other hand, vibrant colors might energize spaces intended for creativity and activity.

Finally, establishing designated areas for specific activities can help cultivate mindfulness by associating certain physical spaces with particular states of mind. Having a dedicated spot for meditation or quiet reading can signal to your brain that entering this space means shifting into a state of mindfulness. This spatial cue helps facilitate the transition from doing to being.

In conclusion, creating a mindful environment is about more than just aesthetics; it's about crafting spaces that align with our intentions for mindfulness practice. Through simplification, connection with nature, thoughtful use of color, and intentional zoning of activities, we can create environments that nurture our mental health and well-being.

4 Mindful Eating and Movement

4.1 Cultivating Awareness in Eating Habits

In the journey towards mindful living, cultivating awareness in eating habits stands as a cornerstone practice that bridges the gap between mindfulness theory and its application in daily life. This practice is not merely about what we eat but how we eat, bringing a level of consciousness to the act of nourishment that often goes unnoticed in our fast-paced world. By engaging fully with the experience of eating, individuals can transform this routine activity into a profound exercise in mindfulness, reaping benefits for both mental and physical health.

The essence of cultivating awareness in eating habits lies in slowing down and paying attention to the sensory experiences involved in eating - the colors, textures, smells, and flavors of food. It's about recognizing hunger cues and fullness signals, thus promoting a healthier relationship with food that transcends automated eating patterns. This mindful approach helps to mitigate mindless snacking, emotional eating, and overeating behaviors that are common pitfalls in modern dietary practices.

Begin each meal by taking a moment to express gratitude for the food before you, acknowledging the journey it has taken from source to plate.

Chew slowly and thoroughly, savoring each bite and paying attention to the subtleties of flavor and texture.

Avoid distractions such as TV or smartphones during meals to ensure your focus remains on the act of eating.

Integrating mindfulness into eating habits also involves making conscious choices about what foods to consume. Opting for nourishing foods that support well-being reflects a deeper level of self-care and respect for one's body. Moreover, this mindful approach extends beyond personal health to encompass ethical considerations about sustainability and the impact of dietary choices on the environment.

Cultivating awareness in eating habits is not an overnight transformation but a gradual process that deepens with practice. It invites us to explore our relationship with food at a more intimate level, opening pathways to greater self-awareness and ultimately contributing to our overall well-being. Through mindful eating practices, individuals can discover a more harmonious balance between nourishing their bodies and nurturing their minds.

4.2 Integrating Mindfulness into Physical Activity

The integration of mindfulness into physical activity is a transformative approach that enhances the connection between mind and body, fostering a deeper engagement with exercise routines. This practice goes beyond the mechanical execution of movements, inviting an awareness that enriches the physical experience and cultivates a sense of presence and focus. By applying mindfulness to physical activities, individuals can unlock new dimensions of their fitness journey, experiencing not only improved physical health but also mental clarity and emotional balance.

Mindful movement encourages participants to tune into their bodies, noticing sensations, breath patterns, and even the flow of thoughts that occur during exercise. This heightened awareness can transform routine workouts into meditative experiences, where each step, stretch, or stroke becomes an opportunity for mindfulness. The benefits of integrating mindfulness into physical activity are manifold; it can enhance performance by improving concentration and reducing anxiety levels, facilitate a deeper connection to the activity itself, and promote a more compassionate self-relationship by acknowledging one's limits and capabilities without judgment.

Begin your exercise session with a few moments of stillness, focusing on your breath to center yourself in the present moment.

As you move, pay close attention to the sensations in your body - the muscle tension, heart rate changes, or any areas of discomfort. Use these signals as guides for adjusting your intensity or form.

End your session with a period of cool-down stretching combined with deep breathing to reflect on your practice and acknowledge your efforts.

Incorporating mindfulness into physical activities does not require drastic changes to your workout regimen; rather, it involves shifting how you approach these activities mentally. Whether you're running, lifting weights, practicing yoga, or engaging in team sports, mindfulness can be woven into any form of exercise. It invites practitioners to experience movement not as a task to be completed but as an enjoyable journey to be savored. Through mindful movement practices, individuals can discover not just greater physical vitality but also emotional resilience and mental clarity.

This holistic approach aligns well with contemporary understandings of wellness that emphasize balance and harmony between mind and body. As we navigate through our fast-paced lives, integrating mindfulness into our physical activities offers a powerful antidote to stress and disconnection from ourselves. It transforms exercise from mere physical exertion into an act of self-care that nourishes both body and soul.

4.3 Mindful Eating for Better Health

Mindful eating is a practice that transforms the act of eating from a routine task into an enriching, conscious experience. It involves paying full attention to the experience of eating and drinking, both inside and outside the body. Mindful eating encompasses noticing the colors, smells, textures, flavors, temperatures, and even the sounds (crunch!) of our food. By engaging in mindful eating, individuals can improve their relationship with food, leading to better health outcomes.

At its core, mindful eating is about using mindfulness to reach a state of full attention to your experiences, cravings, and physical cues when eating. Fundamentally different from dieting, mindful eating is not about restrictions but rather about experiencing food more intensely—especially the pleasure of it. You might find yourself satisfied with less food if you're savoring each bite under a lens of mindfulness.

The practice begins before you eat. By selecting foods that are both nourishing and pleasurable, you set the stage for a mindful meal. This choice itself can be an act of mindfulness, considering where your food comes from and how it will benefit your body. During meals, it helps to eat slowly without distraction (e.g., no screens), chewing thoroughly and pausing between bites to put down utensils. This allows you to fully taste what you eat and listen to your body's hunger cues.

Mindful eating also involves acknowledging responses to food (likes, dislikes or neutral) without judgment. Practicing gratitude for your meal and recognizing the effort that went into its preparation can enhance the dining experience further by connecting you with broader aspects of food production and preparation.

Research suggests that mindful eating can lead to improved digestion since it promotes slower eating which gives your digestive system ample time to process nutrients effectively. Moreover, it has been linked with weight loss as it helps in reducing binge-eating behaviors and promotes a healthier relationship with food.

Incorporating mindful eating into daily life doesn't require drastic changes; start small by focusing on one meal a day or even one snack. Over time as mindfulness becomes more integrated into your meals, you may notice changes in your eating habits naturally aligning with healthier choices because you're paying closer attention to what your body truly needs.

Ultimately, mindful eating is about creating a healthy relationship with food that acknowledges its role as nourishment for our bodies while enjoying every bite taken. It's an approach that encourages listening closely to our internal cues for hunger and satiety instead of external cues like diet trends or societal expectations around what we should eat.

Enhancing Communication through Mindfulness

5.1 Listening with Full Attention

In the bustling rhythm of modern life, where distractions are omnipresent, listening with full attention emerges as a crucial yet often overlooked aspect of effective communication. This practice is not merely about hearing the words spoken by another but involves a deep engagement with the speaker's message, emotions, and intentions. Mindful listening fosters a connection that transcends superficial interaction, paving the way for more meaningful relationships and understanding.

At its core, listening with full attention is an act of mindfulness. It requires us to be fully present in the moment, setting aside our own judgments, preconceptions, and internal dialogues to truly hear what is being said. This form of listening goes beyond passive reception; it is an active process that engages both the heart and mind. By doing so, we open ourselves to new perspectives and insights, allowing for genuine dialogue and exchange.

The benefits of mindful listening are manifold. For one, it enhances our ability to connect with others on a deeper level, fostering empathy and compassion. When someone feels genuinely heard and understood, it builds trust and strengthens relationships. Moreover, this practice can significantly improve our interpersonal skills by reducing conflicts and misunderstandings that often arise from miscommunication.

However, cultivating the habit of listening with full attention is not without its challenges in today's fast-paced world. Distractions such as technology, social media, and our own incessant thoughts can impede our ability to listen mindfully. Overcoming these obstacles requires intentional effort and practice. Strategies such as minimizing external distractions during conversations, practicing active engagement through nodding or verbal affirmations, and regularly reflecting on our listening habits can enhance our capacity for mindful listening.

In conclusion, embracing the art of listening with full attention is a transformative practice that enriches both personal and professional interactions. By committing to being fully present in our conversations, we not only improve our communication skills but also contribute to creating a more empathetic and connected world.

5.2 Speaking with Purpose and Kindness

In the realm of effective communication, speaking with purpose and kindness is as crucial as listening attentively. This approach not only enhances the clarity and impact of our messages but also fosters a positive environment that encourages open dialogue and mutual respect. By integrating mindfulness into our speech, we can ensure that our words are both meaningful and considerate, reflecting a deep awareness of their potential effects on others.

Speaking with purpose involves being clear about what we want to convey before we begin to speak. This requires a moment of reflection to consider the intention behind our message and the outcomes we hope to achieve. Whether it's to inform, persuade, comfort, or connect, having a clear purpose guides our choice of words and the manner in which we express them. It helps us stay focused on the topic at hand, avoiding unnecessary digressions that can dilute the message or confuse the listener.

Kindness in communication goes beyond mere politeness; it embodies empathy, compassion, and a genuine concern for the well-being of others. When we speak with kindness, we pay attention to how our words might be received and make an effort to ensure they uplift rather than undermine. This doesn't mean shying away from difficult conversations or avoiding honest feedback but rather framing our thoughts in a way that is respectful and constructive.

The practice of mindful speaking encourages us to pause before responding in conversations, allowing us time to formulate thoughts that are both truthful and benevolent. This pause can be instrumental in preventing reactive responses driven by emotions such as anger or frustration, which often lead to regrettable exchanges. Instead, it opens up space for thoughtful consideration of how best to articulate our views without causing harm.

Moreover, speaking with purpose and kindness has profound implications for relationship building. It creates a foundation of trust and safety that enables deeper connections with others. People are more likely to listen openly and engage sincerely when they feel respected and valued in conversation. Additionally, this approach can significantly reduce misunderstandings and conflicts that stem from careless or aggressive communication styles.

In conclusion, embracing mindfulness in how we speak transforms not only our interactions but also nurtures healthier relationships both personally and professionally. By committing to communicate with intentionality and compassion, we contribute towards a more empathetic society where meaningful exchanges pave the way for collective understanding and growth.

5.3 Mindful Communication in Relationships

Mindful communication in relationships is a transformative practice that goes beyond the foundational aspects of speaking with purpose and kindness. It involves an intentional approach to how we interact with others, emphasizing the quality of presence, empathy, and deep listening. This mindful approach fosters stronger connections, reduces misunderstandings, and cultivates a nurturing environment where both individuals feel heard and valued.

At the heart of mindful communication is the concept of presence. Being fully present in conversations means giving our undivided attention to the other person, free from distractions or preoccupations. This level of attentiveness signals to our partners that they are important and what they have to say matters. It creates a space where genuine exchange can occur, enhancing intimacy and trust.

Empathy plays a crucial role in mindful communication within relationships. It involves striving to understand our partner's perspective without immediate judgment or trying to fix their problems unless solicited. Empathy requires us to put ourselves in their shoes, acknowledging their feelings and validating their experiences. This empathetic stance fosters emotional connection and shows our partners that we truly care about their well-being.

Deep listening is another pillar of mindful communication in relationships. It extends beyond simply hearing words; it involves listening with all our senses to the emotions and unspoken messages behind those words. Deep listening can help uncover underlying issues or needs that may not be immediately apparent, allowing for more effective problem-solving and support.

Practicing non-reactivity during challenging conversations by taking a moment to breathe before responding.

Expressing gratitude regularly for your partner's actions or qualities, reinforcing positive interactions.

Using "I" statements to express feelings without placing blame, reducing defensiveness.

Incorporating mindfulness into our communication practices requires patience and dedication but yields significant rewards for relationship health and satisfaction. By committing to being present, empathetic, and deeply attentive listeners, we pave the way for more meaningful connections with our partners. Mindful communication thus becomes not just a tool for resolving conflicts but a pathway to deeper understanding and love.

Transforming Work Habits with Mindfulne

6.1 Creating a Balanced Work-Life through Presence

In today's fast-paced world, achieving a balanced work-life is more challenging and essential than ever before. The concept of presence, deeply rooted in mindfulness practices, offers a transformative approach to navigating the complexities of modern living. By cultivating presence, individuals can enhance their ability to remain focused and calm amidst the demands of work and personal life, leading to improved well-being and productivity.

Presence in the context of work-life balance refers to the quality of being fully engaged and attentive in the current moment, regardless of the task at hand. This state of awareness enables individuals to manage their time and energy more effectively, making conscious choices that align with their values and long-term goals. Through presence, one can recognize when work begins to encroach upon personal time or vice versa, allowing for adjustments that foster harmony between these two aspects of life.

The practice of mindfulness meditation is a powerful tool for developing presence. It involves sitting quietly, focusing on the breath or another anchor point, and gently bringing attention back whenever it wanders. This practice trains the mind to stay present, which can then be applied to everyday activities. By integrating mindfulness into daily routines—such as during commutes, meals, or meetings—individuals can maintain a state of presence throughout their day.

Setting clear boundaries between work and personal time to avoid burnout.

Prioritizing tasks based on importance rather than urgency to reduce stress and increase efficiency.

Taking short breaks throughout the day to reset focus and prevent mental fatigue.

Moreover, cultivating presence can transform interpersonal relationships both at work and home by improving communication skills and empathy. When individuals are fully present with colleagues or loved ones, they listen more attentively and respond more thoughtfully, strengthening connections and fostering a supportive environment.

In conclusion, creating a balanced work-life through presence is not only about managing time but also about enhancing the quality of each moment spent working or with loved ones. By embracing mindfulness practices such as meditation and mindful living strategies, individuals can navigate the demands of modern life with greater ease and fulfillment.

6.2 Managing Stress and Enhancing Productivity

In the realm of professional development, managing stress and enhancing productivity stand as pivotal elements for achieving success and maintaining a healthy work-life balance. This section delves into strategies that leverage mindfulness to mitigate stress levels while simultaneously boosting one's efficiency and output in the workplace. The interconnection between reduced stress and increased productivity cannot be overstated; as stress diminishes, cognitive functions such as focus, decision-making, and creativity are significantly enhanced.

Mindfulness practices offer a robust framework for recognizing early signs of stress, allowing individuals to address these symptoms before they escalate into larger issues. Techniques such as focused breathing exercises, guided meditations, and mindful walking can serve as immediate interventions to lower stress in high-pressure situations. These practices not only soothe the nervous system but also redirect attention from distressing thoughts to the present moment, fostering a sense of calmness and clarity.

Moreover, integrating mindfulness into daily work routines can transform one's approach to tasks and time management. By cultivating a mindful presence, individuals become more adept at prioritizing tasks based on value rather than reacting impulsively to urgent but less important activities. This shift in perspective enables more strategic planning and execution of responsibilities, leading to higher productivity levels without the accompanying burnout.

Implementing regular mindfulness breaks throughout the day to reset attention and refresh mental energy.

Practicing mindful listening during meetings and interactions with colleagues to improve communication effectiveness and reduce misunderstandings.

Setting intentions at the start of each day or task to foster a focused and purpose-driven approach to work.

The benefits of managing stress through mindfulness extend beyond individual well-being; they contribute to a more harmonious workplace environment where collaboration thrives. Teams that practice mindfulness collectively report improved morale, greater empathy among members, and enhanced problem-solving capabilities. Ultimately, by adopting mindfulness strategies for stress management and productivity enhancement, professionals can achieve not only superior performance outcomes but also a deeper sense of satisfaction in their careers.

In conclusion, navigating the complexities of modern professional life demands innovative approaches to maintaining mental health and optimizing work output. Mindfulness emerges as a powerful ally in this endeavor, offering tools that not only combat stress but also elevate productivity through improved focus, resilience, and strategic thinking. Embracing these practices can lead individuals toward a more balanced, fulfilling career journey.

6.3 Mindful Leadership and Teamwork

The concept of mindful leadership and teamwork extends the principles of mindfulness into the realms of leadership practices and collaborative efforts within organizations. At its core, mindful leadership embodies the practice of self-awareness, presence, and compassion in guiding teams towards achieving their goals. This approach not only enhances individual well-being but also fosters a culture of respect, empathy, and open communication among team members.

Mindful leadership involves leaders who are fully present and engaged with their teams, demonstrating an ability to listen deeply without judgment. This level of attentiveness allows leaders to make more informed decisions, recognize the contributions of team members more accurately, and provide constructive feedback that supports growth and development. Furthermore, by embodying mindfulness themselves, leaders set a powerful example for their teams, encouraging a work environment where stress is managed more effectively, creativity is nurtured, and resilience is built.

On the teamwork front, mindfulness encourages a collective sense of focus and unity. Teams that practice mindfulness together can achieve higher levels of communication clarity and reduce conflict through enhanced emotional intelligence. The practice enables team members to approach challenges with a calm mind and a problem-solving attitude rather than reacting impulsively under pressure. This shift in dynamics leads to improved collaboration, innovation, and efficiency within teams.

Conducting regular mindfulness sessions to enhance team cohesion and reduce workplace stress.

Encouraging open dialogues where team members feel heard and valued, thereby strengthening trust within the team.

Implementing mindful listening exercises during meetings to ensure all voices are acknowledged and considered in decision-making processes.

In conclusion, mindful leadership and teamwork represent transformative approaches that can significantly enhance organizational culture by promoting well-being at both individual and collective levels. By fostering environments where people feel supported both emotionally and professionally, organizations can unlock unprecedented levels of engagement, performance excellence, and innovation.

Incorporating mindfulness into leadership styles transforms traditional hierarchical relationships into partnerships based on mutual respect and understanding. Leaders become facilitators who empower their teams by recognizing each member's unique strengths while guiding them towards common objectives with empathy and clarity. Similarly, when teams operate mindfully, they navigate obstacles more smoothly due to increased adaptability, shared responsibility for outcomes, and a strong sense of collective purpose.

Nurturing Relationships through Mindful Practice

7.1 Deepening Connections with Others

In the fast-paced world we inhabit, the art of forming and nurturing deep connections with others is often sidelined. The essence of mindfulness, as explored in "Mindful Living: Cultivating Inner Peace in a Busy World," offers invaluable insights into how we can enhance our relationships through intentional presence and empathy. This section delves into practical strategies for deepening our connections with others, emphasizing the importance of mindful communication, active listening, and emotional intelligence.

Mindful communication is more than just an exchange of words; it's about being fully present with another person, free from distractions or preconceived notions. It involves listening with full attention and responding with thoughtfulness, thereby fostering a deeper understanding and connection. Active listening further enhances this process by encouraging us to absorb not just the words but also the emotions behind them. This level of engagement shows care and respect for the speaker, making them feel valued and understood.

Emotional intelligence plays a crucial role in deepening connections. It allows us to recognize and manage our own emotions while also empathizing with others'. By developing emotional intelligence, we become more adept at navigating complex social situations and resolving conflicts amicably. This skill is particularly beneficial in maintaining healthy relationships both personally and professionally.

Practicing non-judgmental awareness in conversations to foster openness and trust.

Engaging in shared activities that encourage mindfulness, such as meditation groups or mindful walking, to strengthen bonds through common experiences.

Expressing gratitude openly to reinforce positive interactions and mutual appreciation.

To truly deepen connections with others, it's essential to cultivate a compassionate mindset that prioritizes understanding over judgment. By integrating these mindful practices into our daily interactions, we not only enrich our own lives but also contribute positively to the lives of those around us. Embracing mindfulness as a tool for enhancing relationships enables us to navigate the complexities of human connections with grace and empathy, leading to more meaningful and fulfilling interactions.

7.2 Handling Conflicts with Compassion

In the journey of nurturing relationships, conflicts are inevitable. However, the manner in which we handle these disagreements can significantly impact the strength and longevity of our connections. Embracing compassion as a cornerstone for resolving conflicts not only facilitates healing but also deepens mutual understanding and respect. This section explores the transformative power of compassionate conflict resolution and offers practical strategies for applying it in our daily interactions.

At its core, handling conflicts with compassion involves recognizing the shared humanity between ourselves and others, even in moments of disagreement. It requires us to step back from our immediate reactions or the need to be right, and instead, approach the situation with empathy, openness, and a genuine desire for resolution. This mindset shift is crucial for moving beyond surface-level arguments to addressing underlying needs and emotions that may be fueling the conflict.

One effective strategy is active listening. This goes beyond merely hearing words; it's about fully engaging with the other person's perspective without judgment or interruption. By doing so, we signal that their feelings and viewpoints are valid and important, which can significantly reduce defensiveness and open up space for constructive dialogue.

Another key aspect is expressing oneself honestly but gently. Using "I" statements allows us to convey our own feelings and needs without blaming or criticizing the other person. For example, saying "I feel upset when..." instead of "You always..." helps keep the focus on resolving the issue rather than escalating blame.

Practicing patience by giving each other time to speak without rushing to conclusions or solutions.

Seeking common ground instead of focusing solely on differences.

Agreeing to take a break if emotions become too intense, ensuring that conversations resume in a calmer state.

Incorporating mindfulness into conflict resolution can further enhance compassionate handling of disagreements. Mindfulness encourages us to remain present and aware during difficult conversations, allowing us to choose responses that align with our values rather than reacting impulsively out of anger or frustration.

To truly embrace compassion in conflict resolution is to recognize that every conflict presents an opportunity for growth, learning, and deeper connection. By approaching disagreements with empathy, patience, and openness, we pave the way for more meaningful relationships built on mutual respect and understanding.

7.3 Building Empathy and Understanding

In the realm of nurturing relationships, the development of empathy and understanding stands as a pivotal cornerstone. This process involves more than merely recognizing emotions in others; it requires an immersive dive into the perspectives and experiences that shape their reality. By fostering empathy, we bridge gaps between differing viewpoints, cultivating a soil rich for mutual respect and deeper connections.

Empathy begins with active listening, a skill that extends beyond the confines of conflict resolution discussed in previous sections. It entails fully immersing oneself in another's narrative without preconceptions or distractions. This level of engagement signals to others that their experiences are not only acknowledged but valued. Such validation can transform interactions, paving the way for genuine understanding and connection.

Another vital aspect is the practice of vulnerability. Sharing one's own feelings and uncertainties can dismantle barriers, encouraging others to open up. This reciprocal exchange deepens bonds, creating a shared space where individuals feel safe to express themselves authentically. Vulnerability acts as a catalyst for empathy, allowing individuals to see reflections of their own struggles and triumphs in others.

To further cultivate empathy and understanding, it is essential to recognize and challenge our biases and assumptions. Each person's worldview is shaped by unique experiences; acknowledging this diversity enables us to approach interactions with curiosity rather than judgment. Asking open-ended questions can facilitate this exploration, inviting stories that illuminate diverse perspectives.

Implementing mindfulness practices also plays a crucial role in building empathy. Mindfulness encourages present-moment awareness, helping individuals tune into not just their thoughts and feelings but also those of others around them. Through mindfulness, one can learn to pause before reacting, choosing responses that foster connection instead of division.

In conclusion, building empathy and understanding within relationships is an ongoing journey that demands intentionality and practice. It involves listening deeply, sharing vulnerably, challenging personal biases, asking questions with genuine curiosity, and embracing mindfulness. These efforts not only enrich personal growth but also weave threads of compassion through the fabric of our interactions, strengthening the collective tapestry of human connection.

8 Advanced Practices in Mindfulness

8.1 Developing Compassion and Empathy

In the journey towards cultivating a mindful life, developing compassion and empathy stands as a cornerstone for personal growth and the fostering of meaningful connections with others. This aspect of mindfulness practice not only enhances our ability to understand and share the feelings of another but also serves as a bridge to deeper self-awareness and inner peace. By nurturing these qualities, individuals can transcend mere self-interest to embrace a more inclusive perspective on human experience.

Compassion involves recognizing the suffering of others and taking action to help alleviate it. It is an active expression of empathy, which is the capacity to understand or feel what another person is experiencing from within their frame of reference. In essence, empathy allows us to 'walk in someone else's shoes,' while compassion compels us to offer support or assistance. These interconnected qualities are essential for building strong, supportive relationships and communities.

The cultivation of compassion and empathy is not always intuitive in today's fast-paced world, where individual achievements often overshadow collective well-being. However, mindfulness practices provide powerful tools for developing these attributes. Mindful listening, for example, encourages us to be fully present with others without judgment or distraction, fostering a deeper empathetic connection. Similarly, loving-kindness meditation extends our natural capacity for empathy into active compassion by encouraging positive wishes for ourselves and others.

Research has shown that engaging in practices aimed at enhancing compassion can lead to significant changes in the brain associated with happiness, emotional regulation, and stress reduction. Moreover, these practices have been linked with increased prosocial behaviors—actions intended to benefit others—thereby contributing to more harmonious social environments.

Incorporating mindfulness techniques focused on developing compassion and empathy into daily routines can transform how we relate to ourselves and those around us. By doing so, we not only enrich our own lives but also contribute positively to the broader community. The path towards compassionate living begins with small steps: acknowledging common humanity, practicing non-judgmental awareness, and choosing kindness in our interactions.

Ultimately, embracing compassion and empathy through mindfulness leads us towards a more fulfilling existence—one marked by deep connections with others and a genuine commitment to alleviating suffering in all its forms.

8.2 Using Mindfulness to Navigate Difficult Emotions

Mindfulness, a practice rooted in ancient traditions and modern psychology, offers a profound approach to navigating the turbulent waters of difficult emotions. By turning towards our emotions with awareness, curiosity, and non-judgment, we can transform our relationship with challenging feelings such as anger, sadness, fear, and frustration. This section delves into the mechanisms through which mindfulness helps us understand and manage these emotions effectively.

At the heart of mindfulness is the principle of presence—being fully engaged with the current moment without resistance or avoidance. When difficult emotions arise, our instinctive reaction might be to suppress or escape them. However, mindfulness encourages us to lean into these feelings with openness and acceptance. This shift in perspective allows us to observe our emotional responses without being overwhelmed by them.

One key aspect of using mindfulness to navigate difficult emotions is the practice of labeling. By simply naming our emotions as they arise ("This is anxiety," "This is anger"), we create a space between ourselves and our experiences. This act of labeling not only diminishes the intensity of our emotions but also enhances our ability to process them constructively.

Breathing techniques are another cornerstone of mindfulness that aid in emotional regulation. Deep, conscious breathing activates the body's relaxation response, counteracting the stress response associated with negative emotions. Through focused breathing exercises, individuals can anchor themselves in the present moment, gaining stability and clarity amidst emotional turmoil.

Body scanning is a technique that involves paying attention to different parts of the body in sequence to identify where emotions are being physically held or manifested.

Loving-kindness meditation extends compassion towards oneself and others, fostering an environment where difficult emotions can be met with understanding rather than judgment.

Mindful walking integrates physical movement with awareness practices offering a dynamic way to process and release pent-up emotional energy.

Incorporating these mindfulness practices into daily life does not mean that we will no longer experience difficult emotions; rather, it equips us with tools to approach them more wisely and compassionately. By cultivating a mindful attitude towards our emotional landscape, we enhance our resilience and capacity for emotional well-being. Ultimately, navigating difficult emotions through mindfulness leads us toward greater self-awareness, inner peace, and fulfillment.

8.3 Cultivating Gratitude and Forgiveness

In the journey of mindfulness, cultivating gratitude and forgiveness stands as a profound practice that not only enhances emotional well-being but also fosters a deeper connection with oneself and others. This section explores the intricate ways in which gratitude and forgiveness serve as essential components of mindful living, offering insights into their transformative power.

Gratitude, at its core, is an acknowledgment of the goodness in our lives. By consciously recognizing the sources of this goodness, both external and internal, we shift our focus from what we lack to what we possess. This shift has a profound impact on our mental health, as numerous studies have shown that gratitude is closely linked with increased happiness, reduced depression, and enhanced resilience. Mindfulness amplifies this effect by encouraging us to live in the present moment, appreciating our current circumstances without longing for more or dwelling on the past.

Forgiveness, on the other hand, involves releasing resentment or vengeance towards a person or group who has harmed us. It does not mean forgetting or condoning the wrongdoing but rather letting go of its emotional hold on us. Through mindfulness practices, individuals learn to observe their feelings of hurt and anger without judgment, understanding them as natural responses to perceived threats or injustices. This compassionate awareness creates space for healing and eventually leads to forgiveness. The act of forgiving not only liberates one from the burden of negative emotions but also opens up pathways to empathy and compassion towards oneself and others.

Practicing daily gratitude by keeping a journal can significantly amplify awareness of life's blessings.

Meditations focused on forgiveness encourage individuals to confront painful emotions directly yet gently, facilitating emotional release.

Gratitude exercises such as reflecting on three good things each day can rewire the brain to notice positive aspects more readily.

The interplay between gratitude and forgiveness in mindfulness practice offers a powerful tool for personal transformation. By embracing these practices, individuals can cultivate a more compassionate attitude towards themselves and others while navigating life's challenges with grace and resilience. Ultimately, gratitude and forgiveness enrich the tapestry of human experience, weaving threads of joy, peace, and connectedness into the fabric of everyday life.

9 Extending the Practice Beyond the Self

9.1 Impacting the Community Positively

The essence of mindfulness extends far beyond the individual, reaching into the heart of communities to foster a collective sense of well-being, empathy, and connectedness. In an age where societal divisions seem more pronounced, integrating mindfulness practices within community settings can act as a powerful catalyst for positive change. This section explores how individuals can leverage their mindfulness practice to contribute to communal harmony and growth.

Mindfulness encourages a heightened state of awareness and presence, which when applied to community interactions, can enhance understanding and compassion among its members. By embodying mindfulness in daily life, individuals can influence their surroundings subtly yet profoundly. This includes promoting peaceful conflict resolution, encouraging empathetic communication, and fostering an environment where every member feels seen and heard.

One practical application is through organized community mindfulness programs that offer free or low-cost meditation sessions. These gatherings not only provide a space for personal tranquility but also strengthen communal bonds by bringing people together with a shared purpose. Moreover, mindful education initiatives in schools teach children the value of kindness, patience, and self-regulation from an early age, planting seeds for a more compassionate future generation.

Beyond these initiatives, impacting the community positively through mindfulness also means engaging in active listening during discussions about community issues. It involves showing up with an open heart and mind rather than predetermined judgments or solutions. This approach fosters a culture of mutual respect and collaboration that can lead to innovative solutions for complex problems.

Implementing neighborhood mindfulness walks to encourage collective appreciation of the present moment and the local environment.

Creating community gardens where mindfulness practices are integrated into gardening activities, promoting both ecological awareness and social cohesion.

Organizing workshops on mindful listening and communication to improve interpersonal relationships within families and community groups.

In conclusion, extending mindfulness practice beyond the self into the realm of community engagement offers a pathway towards creating more inclusive, supportive, and resilient societies. By cultivating an atmosphere where every individual's well-being is valued, communities can thrive amidst challenges, transforming collective hardships into opportunities for growth and unity.

9.2 Environmental Consciousness through Mindful Living

Mindful living extends its influence beyond the personal realm, fostering a deep connection with our environment. This conscious approach to daily life encourages individuals to consider the impact of their actions on the planet, promoting sustainable habits and ecological awareness. By integrating mindfulness into our relationship with the environment, we not only enhance our own well-being but also contribute to the health and sustainability of our planet.

Environmental consciousness through mindful living involves a shift in perspective—seeing ourselves as part of a larger ecosystem and recognizing that every choice we make has repercussions. This realization can lead to more responsible behaviors, such as reducing waste, conserving resources, and supporting eco-friendly initiatives. Mindfulness practices help cultivate this awareness by encouraging us to slow down, observe our surroundings, and reflect on our interaction with the natural world.

One practical application of this philosophy is mindful consumption. This entails being aware of the lifecycle of products we purchase—from their creation to disposal—and opting for items that are produced sustainably and ethically. It also involves minimizing consumption overall, recognizing that less can indeed be more when it comes to leading a fulfilling life while reducing environmental impact.

Another aspect is mindful eating, which connects us more deeply with the food we consume. This practice encourages choosing local, organic produce, reducing meat consumption, and understanding the environmental cost of food production. By eating mindfully, we not only nourish our bodies but also support sustainable agriculture practices that benefit the earth.

Engaging in community clean-up activities to directly contribute to environmental preservation while fostering a sense of collective responsibility.

Practicing zero-waste living by reducing plastic use and finding creative ways to reuse materials instead of discarding them.

Incorporating green transportation methods like biking or walking for short trips to reduce carbon footprint.

Beyond individual actions, environmental consciousness through mindful living inspires advocacy for broader change. It involves supporting policies and initiatives that protect natural habitats, conserve resources, and mitigate climate change. By raising awareness and influencing others through example, mindful individuals can play a crucial role in driving societal shifts towards sustainability.

In conclusion, environmental consciousness through mindful living offers a path toward harmonizing human existence with nature's rhythms. It challenges us to rethink our lifestyles and make choices that promote ecological balance. Through mindfulness, we can transform our relationship with the environment from one of exploitation to one of stewardship—a critical step in ensuring a healthy planet for future generations.

9.3 Mindfulness in Education and Social Change

The integration of mindfulness into education and its role in fostering social change represents a significant shift towards more empathetic, aware, and sustainable societies. By embedding mindfulness practices within the educational system, students are not only equipped with tools for personal well-being but are also prepared to engage with the world around them in a more conscious and constructive manner. This approach has the potential to reshape educational paradigms, promoting a culture of peace, empathy, and global citizenship.

Mindfulness in education goes beyond mere stress reduction or attention enhancement. It introduces a transformative element that encourages students to develop a deep sense of connection with themselves and their environment. This holistic approach fosters emotional intelligence, resilience, and compassion—qualities essential for addressing complex global challenges such as inequality, environmental degradation, and social injustice. By cultivating these skills from an early age, mindfulness education contributes to the formation of individuals who are not only academically proficient but also socially and environmentally conscious.

Furthermore, mindfulness practices within schools can create inclusive learning environments that recognize and respect diversity while promoting mutual understanding among students from different backgrounds. Such environments are conducive to dialogue, collaboration, and conflict resolution

—key components in building cohesive communities and driving social change. Through mindful communication exercises, students learn the importance of listening actively and expressing themselves authentically, enhancing their ability to participate effectively in democratic processes.

The impact of mindfulness on social change is also evident when integrated into community-based programs. These initiatives often target marginalized groups, offering tools for empowerment and fostering a sense of agency among participants. By addressing issues such as trauma recovery through mindfulness-based interventions, these programs contribute to healing at both individual and community levels. Moreover, they inspire collective action towards creating more equitable and sustainable societies.

In conclusion, the role of mindfulness in education extends far beyond personal benefits; it is a powerful catalyst for social transformation. By nurturing mindful awareness among young people, educators lay the groundwork for future generations characterized by compassion, empathy, and a deep commitment to positive change. As this practice continues to gain momentum across educational settings worldwide it promises not only to enhance individual well-being but also to propel us towards a more just and harmonious global community.

Special Techniques and Approaches in Mindful Li

10.1 Exploring Various Meditation Techniques

In the quest for inner peace and mental clarity, meditation emerges as a cornerstone practice within mindful living. The diversity of meditation techniques available today offers a rich tapestry of practices that cater to different preferences, lifestyles, and objectives. This exploration delves into the variety of these techniques, shedding light on their unique characteristics and benefits.

Meditation practices can be broadly categorized into two main types: concentrative and mindfulness-based techniques. Concentrative meditation focuses on directing attention towards a single point of reference, such as the breath, a mantra, or an image. This singular focus aims to cultivate a deep state of mental tranquility and concentration. Mindfulness-based techniques, on the other hand, encourage an open awareness of all aspects of experience in the present moment without attachment or judgment.

One popular form of concentrative meditation is *Transcendental Meditation (TM)*, which involves silently repeating a personalized mantra as a means to settle the mind into a state of profound rest and relaxation. Another technique is **Zazen**, or seated Zen meditation, which emphasizes sitting in upright posture and observing the breath or contemplating koans (paradoxical anecdotes or riddles) to foster insight and enlightenment.

Beyond these traditional forms are modern adaptations like *Mindfulness-Based Stress Reduction (MBSR)*, which combines mindfulness meditation and yoga exercises to reduce stress; and *Mindfulness-Based Cognitive Therapy (MBCT)*, which integrates mindfulness practices with cognitive behavioral strategies to prevent depressive relapse.

Vipassana Meditation, also known as Insight Meditation, is a mindfulness-based practice that teaches practitioners to observe bodily sensations, thoughts, and emotions with detachment and equanimity.

Metta Meditation (Loving-kindness Meditation) encourages an attitude of altruism and compassion by mentally sending goodwill, kindness, and warmth towards others.

Guided Visualization involves following spoken narratives that lead the practitioner through imaginative scenarios to evoke positive feelings and states of mind.

The choice among these varied techniques depends largely on personal preference, goals for practice (such as stress reduction, enhanced concentration, emotional regulation), lifestyle considerations, and sometimes physical ability. Experimenting with different methods can be an enlightening process in itself, offering insights into one's mind-body connection and revealing what best supports one's journey towards mindful living.

In conclusion, exploring various meditation techniques opens up a world where inner peace is accessible through multiple pathways. Whether seeking solace from life's stresses or aspiring towards spiritual growth, there exists a meditation practice suited to every individual's needs—making mindful living an inclusive endeavor that enriches our collective human experience.

10.2 Tailoring Practices to Individual Needs

The journey towards mindful living is deeply personal, and as such, the effectiveness of meditation practices hinges on their alignment with individual needs, preferences, and life circumstances. Recognizing this, tailoring meditation techniques to fit one's unique path becomes a crucial aspect of cultivating a sustainable and rewarding practice. This customization not only enhances engagement but also maximizes the benefits derived from these practices.

Individual needs vary widely based on factors such as personality type, daily routine, physical abilities, and specific goals or challenges being addressed. For instance, someone with a busy mind might find more immediate benefits in concentrative techniques that help focus and quieten mental chatter. Conversely, individuals facing emotional turmoil may benefit from mindfulness-based approaches that teach non-judgmental awareness and acceptance of present-moment experiences.

Lifestyle considerations also play a significant role in selecting suitable meditation practices. People with demanding schedules may prefer shorter, more flexible techniques like mindful breathing exercises that can be integrated into daily activities without requiring extended periods of time. Meanwhile, those who can dedicate a set time for meditation might explore deeper practices such as Zazen or Vipassana.

Physical ability is another critical factor; certain health conditions or mobility issues may make traditional seated meditations uncomfortable or impractical. In such cases, adapted practices like walking meditation or chair yoga can offer accessible alternatives that still provide profound mental and physical benefits.

To effectively tailor meditation practices to individual needs, experimentation is key. Trying out different techniques under the guidance of experienced practitioners or through reputable sources can help identify what resonates best with one's personal inclinations and life situation. It's also beneficial to approach this exploration with an open mind and patience, understanding that preferences may evolve over time as one progresses along their mindfulness journey.

In conclusion, the art of tailoring meditation practices to individual needs is fundamental in fostering a meaningful connection to mindful living. By honoring personal differences and embracing flexibility in practice, individuals can discover the most supportive path towards inner peace and well-being.

10.3 Mindfulness in Daily Activities

Mindfulness in daily activities transforms ordinary tasks into moments of deep awareness, offering a pathway to presence and centeredness amidst the hustle of everyday life. This practice involves bringing a quality of attention and intention to our actions, often overlooked in the pursuit of productivity and efficiency. By integrating mindfulness into routine activities, we cultivate a state of being that enriches our experience of the present moment, fostering a sense of peace and fulfillment that transcends the boundaries of formal meditation.

The essence of mindfulness in daily activities lies in its simplicity and accessibility. Unlike structured meditation practices that may require specific postures or controlled environments, mindfulness can be woven into any activity, from washing dishes to walking to work. This seamless integration encourages a continuous flow of awareness throughout the day, blurring the lines between meditation and living. It is here, in the ordinariness of life, that mindfulness reveals its transformative power.

Engaging mindfully with daily tasks begins with intention. Setting an intention to be present during an activity primes our mind for awareness. It acts as a gentle reminder to return to the present whenever we notice our thoughts drifting to past worries or future anxieties. This practice is not about achieving perfection but rather about recognizing and embracing each moment with compassion and curiosity.

Conscious Breathing: Incorporating conscious breaths while performing tasks can anchor us in the present moment, serving as a bridge between mind and body.

Sensory Engagement: Paying close attention to sensory experiences—such as the feel of water on skin while washing hands or the sound of leaves rustling during a walk—enriches our perception and grounds us in now.

Gratitude Practice: Infusing activities with gratitude by acknowledging the value and opportunity they provide fosters a positive mindset and deepens our connection to everyday life.

Mindfulness in daily activities offers an expansive field for practice beyond conventional meditation cushions or yoga mats. It invites us into an experiential journey where every action becomes an opportunity for awakening. By embracing this approach, we not only enhance our own well-being but also contribute positively to those around us through increased patience, empathy, and kindness. Thus, mindfulness becomes not just a personal practice but a way of being that enriches our lives and communities.

1 Overcoming Obstacles in Advanced Practi

1.1 Dealing with Plateaus in Practice

In the journey of personal and professional development, encountering plateaus is a common yet often frustrating experience. These are periods where progress seems to stall, despite consistent effort and dedication to practice. Understanding how to navigate these standstills is crucial for anyone looking to cultivate a deeper sense of mindfulness and enhance their overall well-being.

Plateaus in practice can serve as important indicators that our current methods need reassessment. They challenge us to look beyond our routine strategies and explore new avenues for growth. This phase requires a shift in perspective, recognizing that plateaus are not signs of failure but opportunities for deeper exploration and learning.

One effective approach to overcoming plateaus is diversifying one's practice. This might involve integrating different mindfulness techniques, such as varying meditation styles or incorporating mindful walking into one's routine. Such variations can reinvigorate one's practice, introducing fresh stimuli that encourage mental and emotional growth.

Another key strategy is setting new, achievable goals that align with one's core values and long-term vision. Goals should be specific, measurable, attainable, relevant, and time-bound (SMART). By refining our objectives, we can reignite our motivation and find new directions for advancement.

In conclusion, dealing with plateaus in practice demands patience, openness to change, and a willingness to experiment with new strategies. By embracing these periods as integral parts of the growth process, individuals can uncover deeper layers of insight within their mindfulness journey. Overcoming plateaus not only revitalizes one's practice but also strengthens resilience and adaptability—qualities essential for navigating the complexities of modern life.

Engaging with a community or seeking mentorship can provide support and fresh perspectives.

Reflecting on one's journey through journaling or mindful conversation can uncover hidden insights that propel us forward.

Incorporating restorative practices like yoga or tai chi can enhance physical awareness and mental clarity, aiding in overcoming stagnation.

11.2 Addressing Advanced Challenges

In the realm of personal and professional development, advanced challenges often emerge as one progresses further in their journey. These challenges are multifaceted and require a nuanced approach to overcome. They test our resilience, adaptability, and depth of understanding, pushing us beyond the comfort zones established by earlier successes. Addressing these advanced challenges is pivotal for sustained growth and achieving higher levels of mastery.

Advanced challenges often manifest as complex problems that lack straightforward solutions. They may involve navigating intricate dynamics within professional environments, or they might pertain to deep-seated personal barriers that resist conventional approaches. The key to addressing these challenges lies in developing a strategic mindset that embraces complexity and uncertainty as opportunities for innovation and deeper insight.

To effectively tackle advanced challenges, it's essential to cultivate a robust support network that includes mentors, peers, and professionals who can offer guidance, feedback, and different perspectives. This network serves as a valuable resource for brainstorming solutions, gaining new knowledge, and staying motivated in the face of adversity.

Another critical aspect is fostering mental agility—the ability to quickly adapt one's thinking and strategies in response to changing circumstances. This involves being open to experimenting with new methods, learning from failures without becoming discouraged, and continuously seeking out new knowledge to expand one's skill set.

In conclusion, addressing advanced challenges requires a holistic approach that combines strategic thinking with personal growth initiatives. By leveraging support networks, embracing mental agility, engaging in reflective practices, continually learning new skills, and prioritizing self-care, individuals can navigate complex obstacles more effectively. Overcoming these hurdles not only leads to professional advancement but also contributes significantly to personal fulfillment and resilience.

Engaging in reflective practice is crucial for identifying underlying patterns that contribute to persistent challenges. This can involve journaling about experiences, meditating on obstacles faced, or discussing issues with trusted advisors.

Investing time in learning advanced techniques relevant to one's field can provide fresh approaches to old problems. Whether through formal education or self-directed study, expanding one's toolkit is invaluable.

Prioritizing self-care is also fundamental when addressing advanced challenges. High levels of stress can impede creative thinking and problem-solving abilities; therefore, incorporating activities that promote physical well-being and mental health is essential.

11.3 Maintaining Motivation and Consistency

Maintaining motivation and consistency is a critical aspect of overcoming obstacles in advanced practice. As individuals progress in their personal and professional development, the initial burst of enthusiasm can wane, faced with the reality of persistent challenges and the requirement for sustained effort. This section delves into strategies for keeping motivation high and ensuring consistent progress towards goals, even when faced with complex problems that demand a sophisticated approach.

The journey towards mastery in any field is marred by periods of stagnation, frustration, and doubt. These emotional responses can derail one's progress, making it essential to develop mechanisms for sustaining motivation over long periods. One effective strategy is setting clear, achievable goals that provide direction and a sense of purpose. These goals act as milestones on the path to mastery, offering tangible evidence of progress even when the end seems distant.

Another key element in maintaining motivation is fostering a growth mindset—the belief that abilities can be developed through dedication and hard work. This perspective encourages resilience in the face of challenges, viewing them as opportunities to learn and grow rather than insurmountable barriers. Embracing this mindset helps individuals persevere when they encounter setbacks, maintaining their focus on long-term objectives rather than becoming mired in temporary failures.

Consistency in practice is equally important; it builds competence and confidence over time. Developing a routine or schedule that dedicates regular time to focused practice or study can help embed this consistency. However, it's crucial to balance discipline with flexibility—allowing for adjustments based on feedback and changing circumstances without losing sight of overall goals.

Engagement with a supportive community plays a vital role in sustaining motivation and consistency. Sharing experiences with peers facing similar challenges provides not only emotional support but also practical advice and alternative perspectives that can reinvigorate one's commitment to their journey.

In conclusion, maintaining motivation and consistency requires a multifaceted approach that includes goal setting, cultivating a growth mindset, establishing routines for consistent practice, and engaging with supportive communities. By integrating these strategies into their approach to advanced challenges, individuals can navigate the complexities of personal and professional development more effectively, turning obstacles into stepping stones towards mastery.

2 Continuing the Journey – Lifelong Practi

12.1 Incorporating Lessons into Daily Life

In the journey towards cultivating inner peace and enhancing mental well-being, incorporating the lessons of mindfulness into daily life stands as a pivotal step. This process involves more than just understanding or appreciating the value of mindfulness; it requires a deliberate and consistent effort to integrate these practices into every aspect of one's routine. The essence of this integration lies in transforming ordinary activities into opportunities for mindfulness practice, thereby fostering a continuous state of awareness and presence.

The challenge many face is not in grasitating the concepts of mindfulness but in finding practical ways to weave these principles into the fabric of their busy lives. It begins with recognizing that every moment holds potential for mindfulness practice. From mindful eating, where attention is given to the experience of eating, to mindful walking, where each step is taken with intention and awareness, opportunities abound for practicing mindfulness throughout the day.

One effective strategy is starting small by selecting one or two activities where mindfulness can be easily applied without overwhelming oneself. For instance, dedicating a few minutes each morning to meditate or simply observe one's breath can set a tone of mindfulness for the day ahead. Gradually, as these practices become ingrained habits, they can be expanded to other areas such as work tasks, conversations with others, and even during leisure activities like reading or exercising.

Identifying moments in daily routines that offer opportunities for mindfulness practice.

Setting realistic goals for integrating mindfulness practices into daily life.

Using reminders or cues to maintain awareness throughout the day.

Beyond individual practices, incorporating lessons into daily life also means adopting an attitude of openness and curiosity towards experiences without immediate judgment. This mindset shift allows individuals to approach situations with a fresh perspective, enhancing their ability to respond rather than react to circumstances around them. As these mindful practices deepen, they not only contribute to personal well-being but also positively influence interactions with others and one's environment.

In conclusion, weaving mindfulness into the fabric of daily life is an evolving process that requires patience and persistence. By starting small, setting achievable goals, and gradually expanding mindfulness practices across different aspects of life, individuals can transform their relationship with themselves and their surroundings. This ongoing journey enriches life with greater clarity, compassion, and connectedness.

12.2 Resources for Further Exploration

The journey of integrating mindfulness into daily life is an ongoing process, enriched by continuous learning and discovery. As individuals seek to deepen their understanding and practice of mindfulness, a wealth of resources stands ready to support this exploration. These resources not only offer guidance and inspiration but also provide practical tools for applying mindfulness in various aspects of life.

Books on mindfulness, written by esteemed authors in the field, serve as foundational pillars for those beginning or continuing their journey. Titles such as "Wherever You Go, There You Are" by Jon Kabat-Zinn and "The Miracle of Mindfulness" by Thich Nhat Hanh offer insights into the essence of mindfulness practice, emphasizing its applicability in everyday situations. These works encourage readers to cultivate a deeper awareness of the present moment, transforming mundane activities into opportunities for growth and reflection.

Digital platforms have also emerged as significant resources for further exploration. Websites dedicated to mindfulness and well-being feature articles, guided meditations, and video tutorials that cater to both beginners and seasoned practitioners. Apps like Headspace and Calm provide structured programs that guide users through various practices, from basic breathing exercises to more advanced techniques aimed at reducing stress and enhancing focus.

Workshops and retreats offer immersive experiences for those wishing to deepen their practice in a community setting. Led by experienced instructors, these gatherings allow participants to disconnect from daily distractions and engage in intensive practice periods. Such experiences often lead to profound insights and a renewed commitment to incorporating mindfulness into one's life.

Lastly, joining local or online mindfulness groups can foster a sense of connection with others on similar paths. Sharing experiences, challenges, and successes with peers can provide encouragement, accountability, and a deeper sense of community.

In conclusion, the path towards integrating mindfulness into daily life is greatly supported by a diverse array of resources. From books and digital platforms to workshops and community groups, these tools offer valuable guidance for individuals at any stage of their journey. By leveraging these resources for further exploration, one can continue to grow in their practice, enriching their life with greater clarity, compassion, and connectedness.

12.3 Sustaining a Mindful Lifestyle

Maintaining a mindful lifestyle is an ongoing journey that requires dedication, practice, and the willingness to continually learn and adapt. It involves more than just occasional meditation; it's about integrating mindfulness into every aspect of your daily life. This commitment can transform how you experience the world, leading to a deeper sense of peace, fulfillment, and connection.

To sustain a mindful lifestyle, it's crucial to establish routines that anchor mindfulness practices in your day-to-day activities. Starting the day with a few minutes of meditation or mindful breathing can set a positive tone for what lies ahead. Similarly, ending the day by reflecting on moments of gratitude can foster a sense of contentment and well-being.

Incorporating mindfulness into routine tasks can also turn mundane activities into opportunities for presence and awareness. For example, paying full attention while eating, walking, or even doing household chores can transform these experiences from being automatic or mindless into rich moments of engagement with the present.

Another key aspect of sustaining a mindful lifestyle is cultivating an attitude of openness and curiosity. Approaching experiences without preconceived notions allows for greater appreciation of the present moment and reduces the tendency to react automatically to situations. This mindset fosters resilience by enabling individuals to respond rather than react to challenges.

Establishing daily mindfulness practices

Integrating mindfulness into routine tasks

Cultivating an attitude of openness and curiosity

Beyond personal practice, seeking out communities or groups focused on mindfulness can provide support and inspiration. Sharing experiences with others who are also committed to living mindfully creates a sense of belonging and can offer new perspectives on deepening one's practice.

In conclusion, sustaining a mindful lifestyle is both rewarding and challenging. It requires consistent effort to integrate mindfulness practices into everyday life but offers profound benefits in return—enhancing one's quality of life through increased awareness, compassion, and connection.

Finally, it's important to be patient and compassionate with oneself on this journey. Progress in mindfulness is not always linear; there will be days when maintaining focus or finding peace seems challenging. Recognizing these moments as part of the process and responding with kindness towards oneself reinforces the principles of mindfulness in action.

"Mindful Living: Cultivating Inner Peace in a Busy World" is a nonfiction book that addresses the increasingly relevant practice of mindfulness in today's fast-paced society. With stress and anxiety levels on the rise globally, this book offers a timely exploration into how mindfulness, rooted in ancient traditions yet prominent in modern wellness practices, can enhance mental health and overall well-being. The book is particularly aimed at individuals overwhelmed by daily commitments, providing them with practical strategies to find inner peace amidst chaos.

The narrative begins by examining the scientific basis of mindfulness, showcasing studies that affirm its positive effects on mental health, focus, and productivity. It then traces the historical evolution of mindfulness from Eastern origins to its current status in Western culture, offering readers a comprehensive understanding of its philosophical underpinnings. Transitioning from theory to practice, the subsequent chapters are devoted to applying mindfulness in various aspects of life such as eating, movement, communication, and work habits. Through exercises, reflective questions, and anecdotes, readers are encouraged to integrate mindfulness into their daily routines.

Addressing common obstacles like time constraints and skepticism towards meditation, the book presents a range of techniques suitable for different preferences. Advanced topics including cultivating compassion and navigating difficult emotions through mindfulness are also covered. This section underscores the potential of extending the benefits of one's mindfulness practice outwardly to positively affect others.

In summary, "Mindful Living" serves as an enlightening guide for those seeking to cultivate inner peace through mindfulness amidst the complexities of modern life. It offers both newcomers and seasoned practitioners valuable insights into making mindful living a transformative part of their everyday existence.

www.ingramcontent.com/pod-product-compliance
Lightning Source LLC
Chambersburg PA
CBHW072000210526
45479CB00003B/1012